UTAH
impressions

photography by Steve Mulligan
and Stephen Trimble

FRONT COVER: The sandstone picture frames of North Window and Turret Arch, Arches National Park. STEVE MULLIGAN

BACK COVER: Onion Creek Rapid on the "Moab daily" river trip, Colorado River. STEVE MULLIGAN

PAGE 1: Reflections, Virgin River Narrows, Zion National Park. STEVE MULLIGAN

RIGHT: Mount Timpanogos, the massive and graceful peak rising to 11,722 feet between Utah and Heber valleys. STEVE MULLIGAN

ISBN 10: 1-56037-258-3
ISBN 13: 978-1-56037-258-5

© 2003 Farcountry Press
Photography © 2003 Steve Mulligan and Stephen Trimble

For more information on our books, write Farcountry Press, P.O. Box 5630, Helena, MT 59604; call (800) 821-3874; or visit www.farcountrypress.com.

Created, produced, and designed in the United States.
Printed in China.

15   14   13   12   11   10   4   5   6   7   8

ABOVE: The Wasatch Range meets the Great Basin and its jewel, the Great Salt Lake, at the mouth of Weber Canyon—the easiest path through the mountains, and so the natural route for highways and railroads bound east from Ogden. STEPHEN TRIMBLE

FACING PAGE: A maze of Navajo Sandstone canyons slice through the Markagunt Plateau, Zion National Park. STEVE MULLIGAN

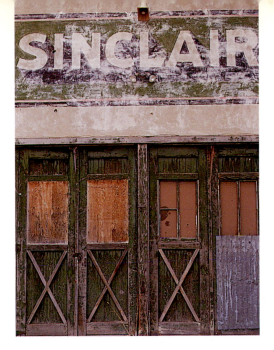

RIGHT: Old service station, Goshen, Utah. STEPHEN TRIMBLE

BELOW: Mule deer in the pioneer Mormon village of Fruita, Capitol Reef National Park. STEPHEN TRIMBLE

FACING PAGE: Lake Powell sparkling below La Gorce Arch in Davis Canyon, Glen Canyon National Recreation Area. STEVE MULLIGAN

ABOVE: Christmas on Temple Square, the Tabernacle and the Temple, Salt Lake City. STEPHEN TRIMBLE

LEFT: Sunset, snow, and salt—Stansbury Island, Great Salt Lake. STEVE MULLIGAN

Hiker approaching the summit ridge, Mount Timpanogos. STEPHEN TRIMBLE

Constantly evolving Park City Resort, from high over the meadows of the Snyderville Basin in a hot-air balloon.
STEPHEN TRIMBLE

ABOVE: Wahweap Marina, Lake Powell, Glen Canyon National Recreation Area.
STEVE MULLIGAN

FACING PAGE: The colorful eroded "sharks' teeth" of the Raplee Anticline,
San Juan River at Mexican Hat. STEVE MULLIGAN

Yellow-blossoming rabbitbrush below the Red Mountains of the
Shivwits Paiute Indian Reservation, west of St. George. STEPHEN TRIMBLE

RIGHT: Collared lizard, Halls Creek, Capitol Reef National Park. STEPHEN TRIMBLE

BELOW: Navajo Indian boy with his family's sheep, Red Mesa. STEPHEN TRIMBLE

LEFT: Hikers in Slickhorn Gulch above the San Juan River, Glen Canyon National Recreation Area. STEVE MULLIGAN

BELOW: Yucca, Island in the Sky, Canyonlands National Park. STEVE MULLIGAN

ABOVE: Small towns celebrate Pioneer Day on July 24 with old-fashioned activities such as this sack race in Bicknell.
STEPHEN TRIMBLE

RIGHT: The lake at Salt Lake City's Liberty Park, precious green space in a busy urban valley. STEPHEN TRIMBLE

The barns of the Huntsville Trappist Monastery nestle in Ogden Valley below the alpine crags of Mount Ogden and Snowbasin Resort.

STEPHEN TRIMBLE

19

RIGHT: Wasatch powder and the wintry face of Mount Ogden, Snowbasin.

STEPHEN TRIMBLE

FAR RIGHT: Wind-blown pine and snowy crags, Red Canyon, Flaming Gorge National Recreation Area.

STEVE MULLIGAN

ABOVE: The West Desert remains largely unvisited, a refuge of space, silence, and solitude for anyone who ventures in to camp in Great Basin ranges like the Barn Hills. STEPHEN TRIMBLE

FACING PAGE: Pool, sun, and fluted sandstone in Fry Canyon—deep within the network of side canyons leading down to the Colorado River. STEVE MULLIGAN

Storm over the La Sal Mountains at sunset,
framed by the state's icon—Delicate Arch,
perched on its sculptured rim of slickrock,
Arches National Park. STEVE MULLIGAN

Queen's Garden,
Bryce Canyon
National Park.

STEVE MULLIGAN

Mount Olympus, guardian mountain of the Salt Lake Valley, brings designated wilderness to the brink of the city.
STEVE MULLIGAN

Historic 25th Street in Ogden, home to the landmark Star Noodle Restaurant (right) and street-fair celebrations of World Cup ski racing at nearby Snowbasin (above).

STEPHEN TRIMBLE

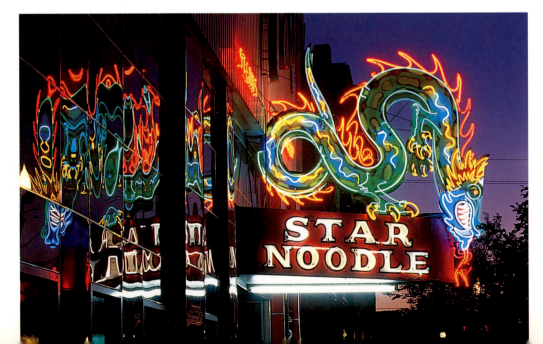

The University of Utah and its wintry backdrop, the Wasatch-Cache National Forest, Salt Lake City. STEPHEN TRIMBLE

ABOVE: Raven tracks in the wet shores of the Muddy River, San Rafael Swell.

FACING PAGE: The confluence of the Green and Colorado rivers, deep in Canyonlands National Park. When John Wesley Powell's men floated onto the Colorado in 1871, they felt they were at last "on the back of the dragon."

The haze of urban Utah veils the wild shores of Antelope Island, Great Salt Lake. STEPHEN TRIMBLE

LEFT: The "urban room," a stunning entrance to Salt Lake City's new library, is a thrilling community gathering place. STEPHEN TRIMBLE

BELOW: Rice-Eccles Stadium was enlarged for the opening and closing ceremonies of the 2002 Salt Lake City Winter Olympics and continues to serve the diehard fans of the University of Utah Utes. STEPHEN TRIMBLE

ABOVE: The ranching culture of the West survives in the sparsely populated counties of rural Utah. Cattle drive, Smoky Mountain Road, Grand Staircase-Escalante National Monument. STEPHEN TRIMBLE

FACING PAGE: The 2,700-foot west face of Notch Peak, in the West Desert's House Range, rises from the floor of the Great Basin Desert. STEVE MULLIGAN

ABOVE: The Six-Shooter Peaks stand as landmark sentinels along Indian Creek, entrance to the Needles area of Canyonlands National Park. STEVE MULLIGAN

FACING PAGE: Frozen potholes atop the sandstone escarpment of Quarry Ridge north of Moab. STEVE MULLIGAN

RIGHT: Water, irresistible in the desert, tumbles into a side canyon of the San Juan River. STEVE MULLIGAN

FACING PAGE: The cycle of sand grains, from ancient desert to towering cliff wall and, now, back to dunes—forming the Coral Pink Sand Dunes near Kanab. STEVE MULLIGAN

ABOVE: The spare beauty of the San Rafael Desert in winter. STEVE MULLIGAN

FACING PAGE: Interstate 70 crosses the face of the San Rafael Reef—an adventure for cross-country drivers and an easy access into the wild country of the San Rafael Swell, a vast unprotected area of public lands with national-park-quality scenery. STEVE MULLIGAN

ABOVE: The adventurous trail to Double-O Arch, Devil's Garden, Arches National Park. STEPHEN TRIMBLE

FACING PAGE: Colorado River at Tilted Park, Cataract Canyon, Canyonlands National Park. STEVE MULLIGAN

LEFT: Mule deer live throughout the state, likely the largest wild animal that visitors will see. STEPHEN TRIMBLE

BELOW: Pony Express riders carried mail across the continent for just two years in the 1860s, but their grit made them part of the lore of America, and lonesome stations like Simpson Springs, in the West Desert, preserve their stories. STEPHEN TRIMBLE

FACING PAGE: Rocky Mountain beeplant, Antelope Island, Great Salt Lake. STEVE MULLIGAN

RIGHT: Slickrock like this trail in Bartlett Wash makes the Moab area the mountain bike capital of the world. STEPHEN TRIMBLE

BELOW: Many Navajo families still live in octagonal hogans like these at Red Mesa. STEPHEN TRIMBLE

FACING PAGE: When the reservoir behind Glen Canyon Dam drops in low-water years, the glorious side canyons return to view. Above Cathedral in the Desert, Clear Creek. STEPHEN TRIMBLE

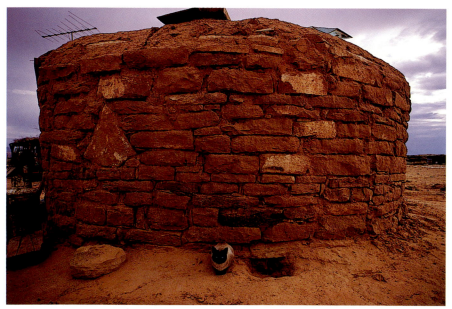

LEFT: Crystallized salt polygons, Bonneville Salt Flats.
STEVE MULLIGAN

FACING PAGE: The rim of the Moab Valley hides the ranks and files of fins of Behind The Rocks, with the La Sal Mountains rolling across the horizon.
STEVE MULLIGAN

ABOVE: Family hiking at Calf Creek, Grand Staircase-Escalante National Monument.
STEPHEN TRIMBLE

FACING PAGE: The Nature Conservancy manages the Matheson Preserve along
the Colorado River at Moab. STEVE MULLIGAN

RIGHT: Prickly pear cactus in bloom, Matheson Preserve, Moab. STEVE MULLIGAN

FACING PAGE: The White River meanders into Utah from Colorado through the remote Uintah and Ouray Ute Indian Reservation. STEVE MULLIGAN

LEFT: A favorite Salt Lake City restaurant housed in an old fire station. STEPHEN TRIMBLE

BELOW: The Sundance Film Festival brings crowds to Main Street in Park City. STEPHEN TRIMBLE

FACING PAGE: Stormlight on Balanced Rock, Arches National Park. STEVE MULLIGAN

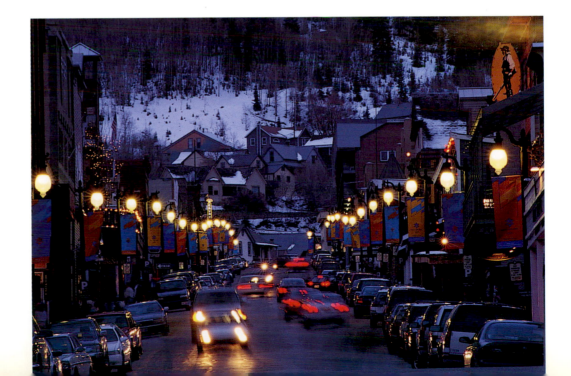

RIGHT: Kayaker in Mile-Long Rapid, Cataract Canyon. STEPHEN TRIMBLE

BELOW: Early fall in the Aspen Giants Scenic Area, Wasatch Plateau. STEVE MULLIGAN

FACING PAGE: Fog hovers over the White Rim, Green River Overlook, Canyonlands National Park. STEVE MULLIGAN

LEFT: Snowbird Resort reflected in the towering windows of The Cliff Lodge. STEPHEN TRIMBLE

FACING PAGE: The rancher who owned Church Rock north of Monticello excavated a room at its base in which to store hay and saddles. STEVE MULLIGAN

LEFT: A desert spiny lizard looks like a lizard should—like a tiny dinosaur! STEPHEN TRIMBLE

BELOW: Escalante retains its pioneer flavor on side streets. STEPHEN TRIMBLE

Goblin Valley State Park—badlands that suit the whimsy and scale of a toddler. STEPHEN TRIMBLE

ABOVE: The wilderness of Grand Staircase-Escalante National Monument can be a stage for children's make-believe; Henry Mountains from Egypt. STEPHEN TRIMBLE

FACING PAGE: Hittle Bottom on the Colorado River, below the Dome Plateau. STEVE MULLIGAN

ABOVE: A field biologist traps an antelope ground squirrel for measurement, Canyonlands. STEPHEN TRIMBLE

LEFT: Fields and a big sky at the Utah Paiute Reservation outside of Kanosh. STEPHEN TRIMBLE

FACING PAGE: The Three Sisters rise in the most famous landscape of spires and buttes— Monument Valley, spanning the Utah/Arizona border. STEVE MULLIGAN

ABOVE: The rocks of Nine Mile Canyon capture the passing of time, from ancient rock art to crumbling rock ranch houses. STEPHEN TRIMBLE

FACING PAGE: Upper Provo Falls on the Mirror Lake Highway deep in the Uinta Mountains, the highest peaks in the state. STEVE MULLIGAN

ABOVE: Dawn over Farmington Bay, along the shorelands of the Great Salt Lake crucial to millions of migrating and nesting birds. STEVE MULLIGAN

FACING PAGE: Fog tumbling over the rim of the Island in the Sky at Half Dome Butte,

ABOVE: *Camarasaurus* skull emerging from the rock, Dinosaur Quarry, Dinosaur National Monument. STEVE MULLIGAN

RIGHT: A weathered juniper on the rim of the Colorado River canyon, Dead Horse Point State Park. STEVE MULLIGAN

ABOVE: Winter patterns in the badlands, Cedar Breaks National Monument. STEVE MULLIGAN

FACING PAGE: Canoeing the San Juan River, Glen Canyon National Recreation Area. STEVE MULLIGAN

ABOVE: Hikers throng to trails in Wasatch-Cache National Forest above the urban terrace of the Wasatch Front; waterfall on the Aspen Grove Trail, Mount Timpanogos. STEPHEN TRIMBLE

FACING PAGE: The cherished wildflower meadows below Devil's Castle in Albion Basin, Little Cottonwood Canyon, Wasatch Range. STEVE MULLIGAN

On the walk to Delicate Arch, hikers rest, silhouetted in an eroded stone window. STEPHEN TRIMBLE

LEFT: Badgers, grizzled digging machines, are a primary predator of small mammals and ground-nesting birds. STEPHEN TRIMBLE

BELOW: Streambanks yield endless patterns of mud and watery reflections, Indian Creek, Canyonlands National Park. STEVE MULLIGAN

ABOVE: The State Capitol rises over the historic Marmalade Hill neighborhood of Salt Lake City. STEPHEN TRIMBLE

FACING PAGE: Rocky Mountain iris and groundsel bloom high in the La Sal Mountains, the highest mountains on the Colorado Plateau. STEVE MULLIGAN

STEVE MULLIGAN is a landscape photographer who operates a stock photography business from his home in Moab, Utah. Using a large format 4×5 camera, he travels extensively, with a particular emphasis on the Utah landscape.

Steve was named by *Outdoor Photographer* as a Master Landscape Photographer and was a columnist for *Camera & Darkroom*. His first book of black and white landscapes, *Terra Incognita*, is out-of-print. A second volume, *EarthWorks*, will be released in late 2003.

PHOTO BY JACOB TRIMBLE

Salt Lake City writer, photographer, and naturalist **STEPHEN TRIMBLE** sunk roots into Utah's slickrock country as a park ranger in the 1970s at Arches and Capitol Reef national parks. His books grew first from this land: *The Bright Edge: A Guide to the National Parks of the Colorado Plateau* and *Blessed By Light: Visions of the Colorado Plateau* (editor). The Great Basin followed: *The Sagebrush Ocean: A Natural History of the Great Basin* and *Earthtones: A Nevada Album* (with text by Ann Ronald). Ten years of fieldwork in Indian Country added *Our Voices, Our Land, Talking With the Clay: the Art of Pueblo Pottery,* and *The People: Indians of the American Southwest.* Exploring the natural world with his wife and two children led to *The Geography of Childhood: Why Children Need Wild Places* (with Gary Nabhan).

Trimble has received significant awards for his photography, his non-fiction, and his fiction—including The Sierra Club's Ansel Adams Award for photography and conservation.